.tiny book of.

TEA & TREATS

HEART SANDWICH COOKIES
page 123

.tiny book of.
TEA & TREATS

Delicious Recipes *for* Special Times

Small Pleasures
· SERIES ·

hm | books

Small Pleasures™
· SERIES ·

hm|books

PRESIDENT *Phyllis Hoffman DePiano*
EXECUTIVE VICE PRESIDENT/CCO *Brian Hart Hoffman*
VICE PRESIDENT/EDITORIAL *Cindy Smith Cooper*
ART DIRECTOR *Cailyn Haynes*
COPY EDITOR *Whitney Law*
CREATIVE DIRECTOR/PHOTOGRAPHY *Mac Jamieson*
SENIOR PHOTOGRAPHERS
John O'Hagan, Marcy Black Simpson
PHOTOGRAPHERS *Jim Bathie, William Dickey,*
Stephanie Welbourne
EXECUTIVE CHEF *Rebecca Treadwell*
TEST KITCHEN PROFESSIONALS
Allene Arnold, Melissa L. Brinley, Kathleen Kanen,
Janet Lambert, Anna Theoktisto, Loren Wood
TEST KITCHEN ASSISTANT *Anita Simpson Spain*
SENIOR DIGITAL IMAGING SPECIALIST *Delisa McDaniel*
DIGITAL IMAGING SPECIALIST *Clark Densmore*

PRESIDENT *Phyllis Hoffman DePiano*
EXECUTIVE VICE PRESIDENT/COO *Eric W. Hoffman*
EXECUTIVE VICE PRESIDENT/CCO *Brian Hart Hoffman*
VICE PRESIDENT/FINANCE *Michael Adams*
VICE PRESIDENT/DIGITAL MEDIA *Jon Adamson*
VICE PRESIDENT/MANUFACTURING *Greg Baugh*
VICE PRESIDENT/EDITORIAL *Cindy Smith Cooper*
VICE PRESIDENT/ADMINISTRATION *Lynn Lee Terry*

Copyright © 2015 by Hoffman Media

Hoffman Media
1900 International Park Drive, Suite 50
Birmingham, Alabama 35243
www.hoffmanmedia.com

ISBN # 978-1-940772-12-7

ON THE COVER: Strawberry Baby Cakes
with Vanilla-Rose Crème (page 100) Recipe
development and food styling by Loren Wood
Photo styling by Lucy W. Herndon

STRAWBERRY BABY CAKES
WITH VANILLA-ROSE CRÈME
page 100

ARNOLD PALMER
page 19

Contents

INTRODUCTION

"There is nothing more satisfying than a cup of tea and treats, especially when shared with someone special."

– PHYLLIS HOFFMAN DEPIANO

FROM THE TIME I had my first cup of tea, I knew that I would always love teatime. I grew up on iced tea, but I never had a cup of hot tea until I was grown. For some reason, it made me feel like a sophisticated British woman, but the truth is it made me realize how lovely it is that anyone can stop and savor a cup of tea.

Steeping your tea with fruits, spices, and other additions is delightful, and flavored hot and cold teas are very popular. Is there anything as warming as hot spiced tea on a cold afternoon or a delicious fruit-infused iced tea in the summer? Both hot and cold teas have their place and can be the highlight of a wonderful gathering.

The creative tea blends that are available today have opened up endless possibilities of mixing flavors together and experimenting with fruit infusions. *Tiny Book of Tea & Treats* is a small collection of ideas for delicious teas, savory appetizers, and tempting desserts. With just a few quick recipes, you can create a special moment for tea and a treat with your friends and family.

Any party can be as formal or as casual as you wish, and this book is filled with ideas to make your gathering memorable for your guests no matter the style. While the more formal teacup and saucer have given way to mugs for outdoor entertaining, your party can be exactly what you envision to suit your lifestyle and setting. And for iced teas, crystal goblets have given way to canning jars for a fun and relaxed tea-party atmosphere.

This book is a resource to help make your entertaining easy. Most of the foods can be made in a short amount of time due to the shortcuts and convenience foods that have been incorporated into the instructions, but the results are still wonderful. The important message that you send to your guests is that they are sharing a moment of time in your life that will be remembered.

Whether you love to host formal teas or casual gatherings, make it your own. Use the cups, glasses, pitchers, and serving dishes that you love. It is an offering of your time and love that will draw people to your table. For these are the times that will make beautiful memories.

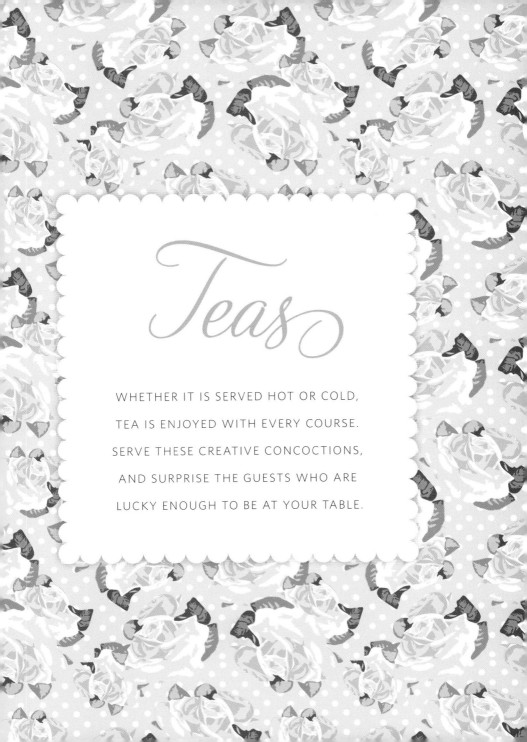

Teas

WHETHER IT IS SERVED HOT OR COLD,
TEA IS ENJOYED WITH EVERY COURSE.
SERVE THESE CREATIVE CONCOCTIONS,
AND SURPRISE THE GUESTS WHO ARE
LUCKY ENOUGH TO BE AT YOUR TABLE.

Apple-Lemon Tea

MAKES 1 GALLON

6 cups water
3 family-size tea bags
½ cup sugar
1 (64-ounce) bottle apple cider
1 (12-ounce) can frozen lemonade concentrate, thawed

In a large Dutch oven, bring 6 cups water to a boil over high heat. Remove from heat, and add tea bags. Cover, and steep for 5 minutes.

Remove tea bags, and add sugar, stirring until sugar is dissolved. Add apple cider and lemonade concentrate, stirring to combine well. Serve chilled or over ice.

Who can resist a brisk glass of tea, especially when apple cider and lemonade are incorporated into the brew? Apple cider, while traditionally served warm, can be served cold as well. The lemonade adds a wonderful citrus infusion to the delightful blend.

Gran's Apple Cider Tea

In a large Dutch oven, bring 6 cups water to a boil over high heat. Remove from heat, and add tea bags. Cover, and steep for 5 minutes.

Remove tea bags, and add sugar, stirring until sugar dissolves. Add apple juice or cider, stirring to combine well. Serve chilled or over ice. Garnish with apple slices, if desired.

Makes 1 gallon

6 cups water
3 family-size tea bags
3/4 cup sugar
1 (64-ounce) bottle
        apple juice or cider
Garnish: apple slices

The apple slices make for a beautiful presentation that will enhance the flavor. Apple cider is made from apple juices that are unfiltered and unsweetened, and it does not contain alcohol unless you choose a variety with it added. For this recipe, either is fine and will result in a delicious tea.

Cherry Tea Cooler

MAKES 16 CUPS

**10 raspberry-hibiscus
tea bags**
10 cups water, divided
1 cup sugar
**10 (¼-inch-thick)
quarter-size slices
peeled fresh ginger**
**6 cups bottled cherry
juice**
**Additional sugar
(optional)**
**Garnish: whole cherries,
mint leaves**

In a teapot or heatproof pitcher, place tea bags. In a medium saucepan, combine 4 cups water, 1 cup sugar, and ginger. Bring to a low boil over medium-high heat, stirring until sugar dissolves. Reduce heat to medium, and simmer, uncovered, for 5 minutes. Remove from heat; remove and discard ginger, and pour over tea bags. Cover, and let steep for 5 minutes. Remove and discard tea bags, and let cool completely (about 1 hour).

In a large bowl, combine tea, remaining 6 cups water, and cherry juice. Cover, and refrigerate for 4 hours or until well chilled.

Serve tea mixture over ice, adding sugar, if desired. Garnish with cherries and mint leaves, if desired.

Fruit teas are very popular when served with a light luncheon. The delicate flavor of cherry juice makes this tea a drink that will delight your guests. Be sure and add a whole cherry to the glass for a splendid touch.

Arnold Palmers

In a medium saucepan, bring 1 quart water to a boil. Remove from heat, and add tea bags; cover, and steep for 5 minutes.

Strain tea into a large container. Add sugar, and stir until sugar dissolves. Add lemonade and remaining 2 quarts water; stir to mix. Cover and chill. Serve over ice. Garnish with lemon slices, if desired.

MAKES ABOUT 1 GALLON

3 quarts cold water, divided
3 family-size tea bags
1½ cups sugar
1 (12-ounce) can frozen lemonade concentrate, thawed
Garnish: fresh lemon slices

" *My wife made a lot of iced tea for lunch, and I said, 'Hey babe, I've got an idea. You make the iced tea and make a big pitcher, and we'll just put a little lemonade in it and see how that works.' We mixed it up, and I got the solution about where I wanted it, and I put the lemonade in it. I had it for lunch after working on the golf course. I thought, 'Boy, this is great. I'm going to take it when I play golf. I'm going to take a thermos of iced tea and lemonade.'* "

– ARNOLD PALMER

Lemon Tea

MAKES 6 TO 8 SERVINGS

6 cups water
3 family-size tea bags
1 (12-ounce) can frozen
   lemonade
   concentrate, thawed
1 cup sugar
½ teaspoon almond
   extract
Garnish: lemon slices

In a small saucepan, bring 6 cups water to a boil. Add tea bags; remove from heat, and let steep for 20 minutes. Discard tea bags.

In a pitcher or serving bowl, combine tea, lemonade concentrate, sugar, almond extract, and enough water to make 1 gallon; stir. Garnish with lemon slices, if desired.

Lemon is the usual accompaniment to iced tea, but a tiny dash of almond flavoring makes this drink even more enjoyable. Find an antique pitcher for your party, and present this delicious drink in a very beautiful way.

Hot Spiced Tea

In a Dutch oven, combine 8 cups water, allspice, cloves, and cinnamon sticks. Bring to a boil over medium-high heat.

Add tea bags, and reduce heat to low; simmer for 6 minutes.

Remove tea bags, and add sugar, orange juice, pineapple juice, and lemon juice; simmer for 15 minutes. Remove spices, and serve hot.

MAKES 2½ QUARTS

8 cups water
1½ teaspoons whole allspice
1 teaspoon whole cloves
5 cinnamon sticks
2 family-size tea bags
1 cup sugar
1 cup fresh orange juice
¾ cup pineapple juice
⅓ cup fresh lemon juice

Hot spiced tea is fitting for a cozy afternoon tea. The combination of spices and fruit juices added to brewed tea is amazing. The tiny lemon slice adorned with whole cloves floats in the cup of tea for a great finishing touch.

Orange-Almond Tea

MAKES 12 CUPS

3 quarts water
3 family-size tea bags
1½ cups sugar
¼ cup frozen orange juice concentrate, thawed
1 teaspoon almond extract

In a large pot, bring 3 quarts water to a boil. Add tea bags to water. Steep for 30 minutes. Remove tea bags.

Stir in sugar, mixing well to dissolve. Add orange juice concentrate and almond extract, stirring well.

Cool to room temperature. Chill until ready to serve.

One of the most refreshing drinks you will serve is a tall glass of Orange-Almond Tea. This is a great tea to serve at brunch in addition to afternoon tea parties.

Pear-Honey Tea

In a medium saucepan, bring 1 quart water to a boil; remove from heat. Add tea bags; cover, and steep for 5 minutes.

Strain tea into a large pitcher. Add pear nectar, remaining 2 quarts water, and honey, stirring to mix well.

Serve over ice.

MAKES ABOUT 2 GALLONS

3 quarts cold water, divided
3 family-size tea bags
3 (46-ounce) bottles pear nectar
1½ cups honey

"Pear nectar has a thick consistency that blends with iced tea marvelously. I love pear nectar and love to serve this Pear-Honey tea. The honey sweetens the drink and can be served on the side if you prefer your guests sweeten their own drinks. I like to serve it separately just as I do when paired with hot tea."

– PHYLLIS HOFFMAN DEPIANO

Spiked Sweet Tea

MAKES 1 GALLON

**3 quarts cold water,
divided**
3 family-size tea bags
½ cup fresh mint leaves
1½ cups sugar
**1 (12-ounce) can frozen
pink lemonade
concentrate, thawed**
**1 cup citrus-flavored
vodka**
**Garnish: fresh lemon
slices, fresh mint
sprigs**

In a medium saucepan, bring 1 quart water to a boil. Remove from heat, and add tea bags and mint; cover, and steep for 5 minutes.

Strain tea into a large container. Add sugar, stirring until sugar is dissolved.

Add lemonade, vodka, and remaining 2 quarts water; stir to mix. Cover and chill. Serve over ice. Garnish with lemon slices and mint, if desired.

Pink lemonade adds a splash of color to this tea. This easy-to-blend drink takes iced tea to a new dimension with the citrus vodka infusion. Serve this in stemmed glasses for a lovely presentation.

Summertime Sweet Tea

In a medium saucepan, bring 1 quart water to a boil; remove from heat. Add tea bags; cover, and steep for 5 minutes.

Strain tea into a large pitcher. Add Strawberry-Lemon-Mint Syrup and remaining 2 quarts water, stirring to mix well.

Serve over ice. Garnish with fresh strawberries, lemon slices, and fresh mint, if desired.

STRAWBERRY-LEMON-MINT SYRUP In a medium saucepan, combine 2 cups water and sugar over medium-high heat, stirring until sugar dissolves. Add strawberries and lemon zest.

Bring to a boil; reduce heat to medium-low, and simmer for 15 minutes. Remove from heat, and add mint leaves. Cover, and steep for 10 minutes.

Strain syrup, discarding solids, and let cool completely.

MAKES ABOUT 1 GALLON

3 quarts cold water, divided
3 family-size tea bags
Strawberry-Lemon-Mint Syrup (recipe follows)
Garnish: fresh strawberries, lemon slices, fresh mint leaves

STRAWBERRY-LEMON-MINT SYRUP
MAKES 4 CUPS

2 cups water
2 cups sugar
4 cups chopped fresh strawberries
2 tablespoons lemon zest
1 (1-ounce) package fresh mint

Our hearts turn to wonderful fruits and berries in the summertime. For a special garden party, this tea is the ideal offering.

Warm Spiced Orange Tea

8 cups water
3 whole cinnamon sticks
1 teaspoon whole cloves
1 teaspoon ground
   cardamom
2 family-size tea bags
1 cup fresh orange juice
¾ cup sugar
½ cup fresh lemon juice
2 tablespoons honey

In a Dutch oven, combine 8 cups water, cinnamon sticks, cloves, and cardamom. Bring to a boil, and add tea bags; reduce heat to low, and simmer for 5 minutes.

Remove tea bags, and add orange juice, sugar, lemon juice, and honey; simmer for 15 minutes. Remove spices, and serve hot.

"Orange is one of my favorite flavors to add to hot tea. It is aromatic when simmering and beckons guests to my kitchen for their first sip."

– PHYLLIS HOFFMAN DEPIANO

Sweet Raspberry Tea

In a large pitcher, stir together tea, bourbon, liqueur, and lime juice. Refrigerate until chilled.

Add ice to fill serving glass, and pour tea mixture over ice. Top with a few frozen raspberries. Garnish with lime slices and mint, if desired.

Tip: Freeze fresh raspberries in a single layer on a baking sheet. Once frozen, store fruit in freezer in a resealable plastic bag. Add frozen raspberries to keep drinks extra cold and to complete the presentation.

MAKES 8 TO 10 SERVINGS

6 cups sweetened tea
1 cup bourbon
½ cup raspberry liqueur
¼ cup fresh lime juice
1 cup frozen raspberries
Garnish: lime slices,
  fresh mint sprigs

Canning jars have made their way to the table for casual, fun events. This tea is creatively served over ice in a straight-mouth jar that is easy for guests to handle gracefully.

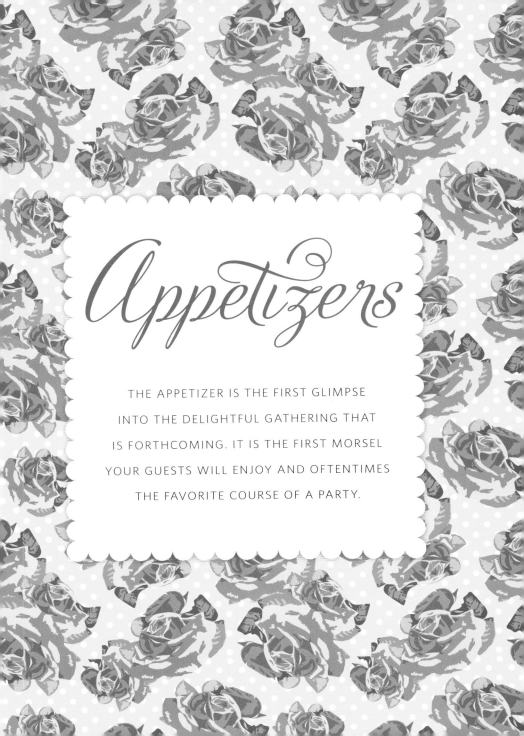

Appetizers

THE APPETIZER IS THE FIRST GLIMPSE
INTO THE DELIGHTFUL GATHERING THAT
IS FORTHCOMING. IT IS THE FIRST MORSEL
YOUR GUESTS WILL ENJOY AND OFTENTIMES
THE FAVORITE COURSE OF A PARTY.

Boursin- and Prosciutto-Stuffed New Potatoes

18 small new potatoes
1 (5.2-ounce) package garlic and herb-flavored Boursin cheese
1 cup chopped prosciutto (about 3½ ounces)
½ cup sour cream
1 tablespoon chopped fresh parsley

Preheat oven to 400°. Line a baking sheet with aluminum foil.

In a large saucepan, place potatoes and water to cover, and boil for 8 to 10 minutes or until fork tender. Drain and let cool.

Cut potatoes in half crosswise; cut a thin slice off round end of each potato to make them level. Using a melon baller, scoop out centers of potatoes, leaving a ¼-inch-thick shell. Place potato pulp in a medium bowl. Add cheese, prosciutto, sour cream, and parsley. Mash with a potato masher until well combined. Spoon mixture evenly into potato shells. Place on prepared baking sheet, and bake for 18 to 20 minutes until lightly browned. Serve immediately.

Small potatoes make excellent miniature baskets for a delightful stuffing when halved and scooped out to form a bowl. These are fantastic, warm appetizers that can be passed to guests who are standing.

Cheesy Bacon-Pecan Spirals

In a medium bowl, combine all cheeses; beat at medium speed with an electric mixer until smooth. Add bacon, pecans, and red pepper. Beat at medium speed with an electric mixer until well combined.

On a lightly floured surface, roll 1 puff pastry sheet into a 13x11-inch rectangle.

In a small bowl, combine egg and water, whisking to combine. Brush egg mixture onto puff pastry sheet. Sprinkle half of cheese mixture over pastry, leaving a ½-inch border. Beginning with short side, roll up jelly-roll style. Repeat procedure with remaining puff pastry and cheese mixture. Wrap tightly in plastic wrap; chill for 2 hours or for up to 2 days, if desired.

To serve, preheat oven to 350°. Line baking sheets with parchment paper.

Cut rolls into ½-inch-thick slices, and place on prepared baking sheets. Bake for 20 to 25 minutes or until golden brown.

MAKES ABOUT 3 DOZEN

2 cups finely shredded sharp Cheddar cheese
1 cup finely grated Parmesan cheese
1 (3-ounce) package cream cheese, softened
1 (1-pound) package hickory-smoked bacon, cooked and crumbled
1 cup finely chopped pecans
½ teaspoon ground red pepper
1 (17.3-ounce) package frozen puff pastry, thawed
1 large egg
1 tablespoon water

Pecans and bacon rolled up with delectable cheeses make splendid pinwheel spirals. Serve them hot right out of the oven with breakfast as well as with tea.

Cranberry Cheese Log with Rosemary and Toasted Walnuts

1 (8-ounce) package cream cheese, softened
2 cups shredded Monterey Jack cheese
1 cup chopped dried cranberries
2 teaspoons chopped fresh rosemary
1 cup chopped toasted walnuts

In a medium bowl, combine cream cheese, Monterey Jack cheese, cranberries, and rosemary. Beat at medium speed with an electric mixer until well combined.

Cover, and refrigerate for 2 hours or until chilled. Shape cheese mixture into a log, and roll in toasted walnuts. Serve with crackers.

Using dried cranberries in a recipe adds fresh flavor and a touch of red. Pecans may be substituted in the recipe if you prefer. Toasting the nuts before using them brings out the flavor.

Creamy Chicken Crescents

In a large skillet, heat olive oil and butter over medium-high heat until butter is melted. Add garlic; cook for 30 seconds, stirring constantly.

Add mushrooms, green onion, red bell pepper, salt, pepper, and garlic powder; cook for 3 to 4 minutes or until lightly browned. Reduce heat to low.

Add cream cheese, stirring until melted. Add chicken, mixing until combined. Remove from heat; cool for 5 minutes.

Preheat oven to 350°. Line a baking sheet with parchment paper; set aside.

Separate crescent dough into 12 triangles; place on prepared pan. Spoon about 3 tablespoons chicken mixture near base of triangle, and roll up, crescent style.

Brush each crescent with melted butter. Sprinkle tops with panko and parsley flakes. Bake for 20 minutes or until golden brown.

MAKES 1 DOZEN

- 2 tablespoons olive oil
- 2 tablespoons butter
- 1 tablespoon minced garlic
- 1½ cups chopped fresh mushrooms
- ½ cup chopped green onion
- ½ cup chopped red bell pepper
- ¾ teaspoon salt
- ½ teaspoon ground black pepper
- ¼ teaspoon garlic powder
- 1 (8-ounce) package cream cheese, softened
- 1½ cups chopped cooked chicken
- 2 (10.1-ounce) cans crescent rolls*
- 2 tablespoons butter, melted
- ¼ cup Italian-flavored panko (Japanese bread crumbs)
- 1 teaspoon parsley flakes

*We used Pillsbury Big and Flaky Crescent Rolls.

Creole Shrimp Bruschetta

1 cup finely chopped
pimiento-stuffed
green olives
1 (7-ounce) jar roasted red
peppers, drained and
finely chopped
¼ cup extra-light olive oil
3 tablespoons red wine
vinegar
2 tablespoons capers
2 tablespoons chopped
fresh parsley
1 teaspoon minced garlic
¼ teaspoon ground
black pepper
24 jumbo fresh shrimp,
peeled and deveined
(tails on)
2 teaspoons Creole
seasoning
2 tablespoons olive oil
24 toasted French rounds

In a medium bowl, combine green olives, red peppers, extra-light olive oil, vinegar, capers, parsley, garlic, and pepper; cover and refrigerate.

In a medium bowl, combine shrimp and Creole seasoning; toss gently to coat shrimp.

In a large skillet, heat 2 tablespoons olive oil over medium-high heat. Cook shrimp for 1 to 2 minutes on each side or until shrimp are firm and pink.

Spoon about 1 tablespoon olive mixture onto each toasted French round. Place shrimp on top of olive mixture.

Standing the shrimp with the tail up creates a lovely presentation and makes it easier for guests to hold the shrimp. If you prefer removing the tail shell, place the shrimp on its side and your guests can enjoy this bruschetta without handling the shrimp.

Tea Biscuits with Herbed Avocado Egg Salad

Prepare biscuits according to package directions. Let cool, and split in half.

Cut eggs in half. Remove 10 yolks, and reserve for another use. In a medium bowl, mash egg whites and remaining 2 yolks using a pastry blender or fork.

Cut avocado in half, and remove pit; scoop out pulp.

In a large bowl, mash half of avocado using a pastry blender or fork. Chop remaining half of avocado, and add to bowl with mashed avocado. Stir in 3 tablespoons mayonnaise, lemon juice, dill, mustard, salt, and pepper. Fold in mashed egg.

On bottom half of each biscuit, spread ½ teaspoon mayonnaise; top each with lettuce, 2 tablespoons egg mixture, and biscuit top. Garnish with fresh dill, if desired.

MAKES 2 DOZEN

24 mini frozen biscuits from 1 (25.1-ounce) package
12 hard-cooked eggs
1 ripe avocado
¼ cup plus 3 tablespoons mayonnaise, divided
1 tablespoon lemon juice
2 teaspoons finely minced fresh dill
2 teaspoons Dijon mustard
½ teaspoon sea salt
½ teaspoon freshly ground black pepper
1 head butter or Bibb lettuce
Garnish: fresh dill

"The convenience of frozen biscuits makes this petite treat easy to make. I always keep a bag of the miniature biscuits on hand and pull out just the number I need at any time."

– PHYLLIS HOFFMAN DEPIANO

Cheese and Bacon Mini Quiche

MAKES 2 DOZEN

1 (14.1-ounce) package refrigerated pie crusts
1 cup shredded sharp Cheddar cheese
½ cup cooked crumbled hickory-smoked bacon
3 tablespoons minced green onion
¾ cup half-and-half
3 large eggs
½ teaspoon dry mustard
¼ teaspoon garlic powder
¼ teaspoon salt
¼ teaspoon ground black pepper

Preheat oven to 350°. Spray a 24-cup mini muffin pan with nonstick cooking spray.

On a lightly floured surface, unroll each pie crust. Using a 2¾-inch round cutter, cut 12 circles from each crust. Press pastry into the bottom and up sides of each muffin cup.

In a medium bowl, combine cheese, bacon, and green onion. Divide bacon mixture among prepared muffin cups.

In a small bowl, whisk together half-and-half, eggs, mustard, garlic powder, salt, and pepper. Divide egg mixture among muffin cups. Bake for 15 minutes or until set. Let cool in pan for 2 minutes. Remove from pan, and serve warm.

No one can resist a warm, cheesy quiche. These delicate bite-size versions are easy to make and will become favorites of your guests.

Gouda Grits Cakes

Line a 13x9-inch baking pan with aluminum foil. Spray foil with nonstick cooking spray, and set aside. In a large saucepan, bring broth to a boil over medium-high heat. Stir in grits, and return to a boil. Cover, reduce heat, and simmer for 5 minutes, stirring occasionally.

Stir in cheese, parsley, and pepper, stirring until cheese is melted. Spoon grits into prepared pan, and spread into an even layer. Cover, and refrigerate for 2 hours or until firm.

Preheat oven to 400°. Line a rimmed baking sheet with aluminum foil, and brush with melted butter. Unmold grits onto a large cutting board. Using a 3-inch round cutter, cut 12 rounds from grits and place on prepared pan.* Bake for 25 minutes. Turn grits cakes over, and bake for 25 minutes more or until lightly browned on both sides.

Top with Scrumptious Shrimp. Garnish with chopped fresh parsley, if desired.

*At this point, grits cakes can be refrigerated for up to 24 hours.

SCRUMPTIOUS SHRIMP In a medium bowl, combine shrimp and seasoned salt, tossing to coat. In a large skillet, heat 2 tablespoons olive oil over medium-high heat. Add shrimp, and cook, in batches, for 1 minute per side or until lightly browned. Remove shrimp to a bowl, and set aside. Repeat with remaining shrimp, adding 2 tablespoons olive oil if needed.

Heat remaining 2 tablespoons olive oil over medium heat. Add green onion, bell pepper, and garlic; cook for 8 to 10 minutes, stirring frequently. Add wine, cream, salt, and pepper; cook for 2 minutes. Add shrimp and parsley, stirring to combine. Remove from heat.

MAKES 12 SERVINGS

6 cups chicken broth
1½ cups quick-cooking grits
1 (7-ounce) package Gouda cheese, shredded
2 tablespoons chopped fresh parsley
¼ teaspoon ground black pepper
2 tablespoons butter, melted
Garnish: chopped fresh parsley

SCRUMPTIOUS SHRIMP
MAKES 12 SERVINGS

1½ pounds large fresh shrimp, peeled and deveined (tails left on)
2 teaspoons seasoned salt
6 tablespoons olive oil, divided
1 cup chopped green onion
1 cup chopped red bell pepper
1 tablespoon minced garlic
¾ cup dry white wine
¾ cup heavy whipping cream
¼ teaspoon salt
¼ teaspoon ground black pepper
2 tablespoons chopped fresh parsley

Herbed Goat Cheese Phyllo Cups

MAKES 2 DOZEN

4 ounces goat cheese, room temperature
4 ounces cream cheese, room temperature
2 tablespoons minced fresh dill
2 tablespoons minced fresh parsley
1 tablespoon minced fresh chives
¼ teaspoon salt
⅛ teaspoon ground black pepper
24 frozen mini phyllo cups, thawed
Garnish: fresh dill

In a small bowl, stir together goat cheese, cream cheese, dill, parsley, chives, salt, and pepper.

Spoon filling into a piping bag fitted with a star tip, and pipe into phyllo cups. Garnish with fresh dill, if desired.

Serve immediately.

Frozen phyllo cups are just asking for a scrumptious filling. Keep these pre-made pastries on hand for when you need to prepare an appetizer in a short amount of time.

Pickled Shrimp

In a small saucepan, combine vinegar, hot pepper sauce, and paprika. Add bay leaves. Cook over low heat for 10 minutes; do not boil. Remove from heat, and set aside to cool.

In a Dutch oven, bring 3 quarts water and 2 teaspoons salt to a boil. Add shrimp; cook for 3 minutes or until pink and firm. Drain shrimp, and set aside to cool.

In a medium bowl, combine vegetable oil, Worcestershire sauce, vinegar mixture, and remaining ½ teaspoon salt.

In a large resealable plastic bag, combine shrimp, onion, and marinade. Seal bag, and refrigerate for 8 to 12 hours, turning occasionally. To serve, remove from bag and discard bay leaves. Serve shrimp at room temperature on saltine crackers.

MAKES 8 TO 10 SERVINGS

- ½ cup distilled white vinegar
- 2 tablespoons hot pepper sauce
- 1 teaspoon paprika
- 10 bay leaves
- 3 quarts water
- 2½ teaspoons salt, divided
- 2 pounds large fresh shrimp, peeled and deveined
- 1 cup vegetable oil
- ½ cup Worcestershire sauce
- 1 large white onion, thinly sliced

Pickled shrimp has more than enough flavor on its own, so feel free to serve it with simple crackers.

Country Ham and Smoked Cheddar Quiche Tartlets

MAKES 6 SERVINGS

1 (2-ounce) slice country ham
1 (14.1-ounce) package refrigerated pie crusts
6 large eggs, lightly beaten
½ cup heavy whipping cream
4 ounces smoked Cheddar cheese, shredded
¼ cup chopped fresh chives
1 teaspoon Worcestershire sauce
¼ teaspoon garlic salt
¼ teaspoon onion powder
¼ teaspoon freshly ground black pepper

Preheat oven to 400°.

In a large bowl, place country ham; fill with warm water. Let stand for 15 minutes to remove saltiness; drain.

Cut ham into ¼-inch pieces, and set aside. Cut 6 (6-inch) circles from pie crusts. Place 1 circle in the bottom of each of 6 (4½-inch) tart pans. Prick bottom and sides of pie crust with a fork.

Place pans on a large baking sheet, and bake for 10 minutes or until lightly browned; let cool completely.

In a medium bowl, whisk together eggs, cream, cheese, chives, Worcestershire, garlic salt, onion powder, pepper, and ham. Evenly divide egg mixture among tart pans.

Bake for 15 minutes or until center is set. Serve warm or at room temperature.

There is nothing quite as comforting as the combination of country ham and Cheddar cheese. And if you throw in a few extra ingredients, you have a treat for all to enjoy.

Pimiento Cheese

In a medium bowl, combine cheeses and walnuts.

Stir in mayonnaise, black pepper, garlic powder, and red pepper. Gently fold in pimientos. Cover and refrigerate.

To serve, spread on sourdough bread, and cut into fingers.

Makes about 4 cups

1 (8-ounce) block white Cheddar cheese, shredded
1 (8-ounce) block fontina cheese, shredded
1 (4-ounce) container goat cheese crumbles
3/4 cup chopped toasted walnuts
1 1/4 cups mayonnaise
1/2 teaspoon ground black pepper
1/2 teaspoon garlic powder
1/4 teaspoon ground red pepper
1 (7-ounce) jar diced pimientos, well drained
Sliced sourdough bread, crust removed

Pimiento cheese makes delicious tea sandwiches when layered on white or wheat bread, and it works great as a snack dip—just use crackers to scoop up every yummy bite.

Roasted Red Pepper
Tea Sandwiches

**2 (12-ounce) jars
roasted red bell
peppers, drained
and divided
1 (8-ounce) package
cream cheese,
softened
1 teaspoon paprika
¼ teaspoon garlic
powder
¼ teaspoon seasoned
salt
24 slices wheat bread
1 cup finely chopped
toasted pecans
Garnish: fresh parsley**

In the work bowl of a food processor, purée 1 jar of drained roasted peppers. Strain purée through a fine-mesh sieve, pressing out liquid with the back of a spoon; discard liquid.

In a small bowl, combine cream cheese, paprika, garlic powder, and seasoned salt. Beat at medium speed with an electric mixer until smooth. Add roasted pepper purée, beating until well combined.

Using a 2-inch square cutter, cut out 48 squares of bread. Using a 1-inch flower-shaped cookie cutter, cut out centers from half of bread squares. Spread cream cheese mixture on one side of whole bread squares. Sprinkle with chopped toasted pecans, and top with bread squares with cutout centers.

Using the flower-shaped cutter, cut out 24 flowers from remaining jar of roasted peppers. Place pepper flowers in center of each sandwich. Garnish with fresh parsley, if desired.

"These tiny tea sandwiches are as tasty as they are bright. And since red is my favorite color, I think the red bell pepper in the center is just the right touch."

– PHYLLIS HOFFMAN DEPIANO

Savory Shrimp Boil Cheesecakes

Preheat oven to 350°.

CRUST In a medium bowl, combine cracker crumbs, Parmesan cheese, melted butter, and egg white, stirring to mix well. Press into bottom and halfway up sides of 2 (12-cup) mini cheesecake pans. Bake for 6 minutes.

FILLING In a medium skillet, heat olive oil over medium heat. Add corn, bell pepper, green onion, and garlic; cook for 3 minutes, stirring frequently. Add shrimp, sausage, salt, and red pepper; cook for 2 minutes, stirring frequently. Remove from heat, and let cool for 5 minutes.

In a medium bowl, combine cream cheese and egg yolks. Beat at medium speed with an electric mixer until creamy. Add shrimp mixture to cream cheese mixture, beating to combine.

Spoon cream cheese mixture evenly into baked crusts.

Bake for 16 to 18 minutes or until set. Garnish with ground red pepper and parsley, if desired.

MAKES 2 DOZEN

CRUST
2 cups firmly packed round buttery cracker crumbs
1 cup finely grated Parmesan cheese
6 tablespoons butter, melted
1 large egg white

FILLING
2 tablespoons olive oil
½ cup fresh corn kernels
½ cup finely chopped red bell pepper
¼ cup finely chopped green onion
1 tablespoon minced garlic
1 cup finely chopped fresh shrimp
1 cup finely chopped smoked sausage
½ teaspoon salt
½ teaspoon ground red pepper
2 (8-ounce) packages cream cheese, softened
2 large egg yolks
Garnish: ground red pepper, chopped fresh parsley

White Barbecue Chicken Bites

**24 (2-inch) rounds white
bread**
¼ cup butter, melted
½ cup mayonnaise
**¼ cup apple-cider
vinegar**
**1½ teaspoons ground
black pepper**
**3 cups shredded cooked
chicken**
**Garnish: fresh chives,
paprika**

Preheat oven to 350°.

Brush both sides of bread rounds with melted butter. Place on a rimmed baking sheet.

Bake for 6 to 8 minutes or until light golden brown.

In a medium bowl, combine mayonnaise, vinegar, and pepper, whisking until smooth. Add chicken to mayonnaise mixture, tossing to coat. Divide chicken evenly among toasted bread rounds.

Garnish with chives and paprika, if desired.

*The taste of a good old-fashioned barbecue
meets teatime with these tangy treats.*

Chicken and Mushroom Tarts

In a large skillet, heat oil and butter over medium-high heat until butter is melted. Add mushrooms and onion, and cook for 5 to 6 minutes or until lightly browned.

Add garlic, salt, and pepper; cook for 1 minute, stirring constantly. Stir in cream cheese until melted. Add chicken, mixing until combined.

Remove from heat, and let cool for 5 minutes.

Preheat oven to 350°. Place phyllo shells on a baking sheet. Spoon filling into phyllo shells, and sprinkle with chives. Bake for 5 minutes.

MAKES 2½ DOZEN

2 tablespoons olive oil
2 tablespoons butter
1 cup chopped fresh mushrooms
½ cup chopped onion
½ teaspoon minced garlic
½ teaspoon salt
¼ teaspoon ground black pepper
1 (8-ounce) package cream cheese, softened
1 cup chopped cooked chicken
30 frozen mini phyllo shells, thawed
2 teaspoons chopped fresh chives

With the crisp shells, rich flavor, and creamy texture, your guests will never guess that these beautiful bites were only in the oven for 5 minutes.

Goat Cheese and Chive Scones

MAKES ABOUT 1 DOZEN

3 cups self-rising flour
½ cup butter
2 (4-ounce) packages
goat cheese
¼ cup finely minced
chives
⅔ cup half-and-half
2 tablespoons butter,
melted

TOMATO RELISH
MAKES ABOUT 1½ CUPS

1 (35-ounce) can Italian
plum tomatoes,
drained
4 shallots, peeled
3 tablespoons
unsulfured molasses,
divided
2 tablespoons olive oil
¾ teaspoon salt, divided
½ teaspoon ground
black pepper, divided
1 tablespoon balsamic
vinegar

Preheat oven to 425°. Line a baking sheet with parchment paper.

Place flour in a medium bowl. Using a pastry blender, cut in butter and goat cheese until mixture is crumbly. Add chives; stir well. Add half-and-half, stirring just until dry ingredients are moistened.

On a lightly floured surface, roll dough to ½-inch thickness. Using a 2¾-inch heart-shaped cutter, cut scones, and place on prepared pan. Bake for 16 to 18 minutes or until lightly browned. Brush with melted butter. Serve with Tomato Relish.

TOMATO RELISH Preheat oven to 350°. Line a 13x9-inch rimmed baking sheet with heavy-duty aluminum foil.

Place tomatoes and shallots on prepared pan.

In a small bowl, combine 2 tablespoons molasses, olive oil, ½ teaspoon salt, and ¼ teaspoon pepper. Using a pastry brush, brush molasses mixture onto both sides of tomatoes and shallots. Bake for 1 hour.

In the work bowl of a food processor, combine tomatoes, shallots, remaining 1 tablespoon molasses, ¼ teaspoon salt, and ¼ teaspoon pepper, and vinegar. Pulse to desired consistency.

Mini Ham and Mushroom Quiche

Preheat oven to 350°. Spray 2 (12-cup) muffin pans with nonstick cooking spray.

On a lightly floured surface, unroll crusts. Using a 3½-inch round cutter, cut 12 circles from each pie crust; reroll scraps as needed. Press crusts into bottom and up sides of each cup of muffin pan.

In a medium skillet, heat butter over medium-high heat until butter is melted.

Add mushrooms, onion, bell pepper, and garlic. Cook for 6 minutes or until liquid is evaporated and vegetables are tender; let cool completely.

In a medium bowl, whisk together eggs, half-and-half, mustard, salt, and pepper until well combined. Divide ham, vegetable mixture, and 1 cup cheese among all prepared crusts. Spoon egg mixture into each crust. Bake for 20 minutes.

Remove from oven, and sprinkle tops of quiche with remaining ½ cup cheese; return to oven, and bake for 5 minutes. Let cool in pans for 5 minutes before removing.

MAKES 2 DOZEN

1 (15-ounce) package refrigerated pie crusts
2 tablespoons butter
2 cups finely chopped baby portobello mushrooms
½ cup finely chopped onion
½ cup finely chopped red bell pepper
2 teaspoons minced garlic
6 large eggs
1½ cups half-and-half
1 teaspoon dry mustard
¾ teaspoon salt
½ teaspoon ground black pepper
1 cup finely chopped ham
1½ cups finely grated Parmigiano-Reggiano cheese, divided

Sweets

SWEETS ARE THE GRAND FINALE OF
A DELIGHTFUL TEA. WHETHER IT IS A
PETITE PASTRY OR A FULL-SIZE SERVING
OF A DELICIOUS TART, THE SWEET
COURSE IS ANTICIPATED BY ALL.

Love-at-First-Bite Macarons

Makes about 3 dozen

**2 cups plus 3 tablespoons
confectioners' sugar**
**1 cup plus 2 tablespoons
almond flour**
5 large egg whites
**⅓ cup plus 1 tablespoon
sugar**
**¼ teaspoon cream of
tartar**
¼ teaspoon salt
1 teaspoon vanilla extract
Edible pearlescent spray*
**Fillings: Raspberry–
Cream Cheese Filling
and chocolate-
hazelnut spread**[†]

RASPBERRY–CREAM
CHEESE FILLING
Makes about 2 cups

**2 ounces cream cheese,
softened**
½ cup fresh raspberries
**3½ cups confectioners'
sugar**

*We used Wilton Pearl Color
Mist Food Color Spray.*

[†]*We used Nutella.*

Preheat oven to 300°. Line baking sheets with parchment paper.

In a small bowl, whisk together confectioners' sugar and almond flour until combined.

In the bowl of a stand mixer fitted with the whisk attachment, beat egg whites, sugar, cream of tartar, and salt at medium speed until foamy. Increase speed to high, and beat until very stiff peaks form. Wait 15 seconds, then beat in vanilla. Stir in confectioners' sugar mixture until blended. Batter should have some fluidity but should not be runny.

Using a pastry bag fitted with a large round tip, pipe batter in 1-inch circles onto prepared pans. Tap pans on counter to release air bubbles. Let pans stand at room temperature for 30 minutes before baking.

Bake for 16 to 18 minutes or until macarons are lightly golden. (Macarons should release easily from the parchment paper. If they do not, they are not done.) Let cool completely on wire racks.

Mist cookies with edible pearlescent spray. Let dry completely. Spread or pipe raspberry-cream cheese filling or chocolate-hazelnut spread on the flat sides of half of cookies. Top with remaining cookies, flat sides down. Serve immediately, or refrigerate for up to 24 hours.

RASPBERRY–CREAM CHEESE FILLING In a medium bowl, beat cream cheese and raspberries at medium speed with an electric mixer until blended. Add confectioners' sugar, and beat until smooth.

Lemon Bars with Browned Butter Crust

Line a 9-inch square baking pan with nonstick or heavy-duty aluminum foil, allowing foil to extend 3 inches over edges of pan. Butter the foil; set aside.

CRUST In a medium saucepan over medium-high heat, melt butter; cook until browned, 4 to 5 minutes. (Watch carefully as butter starts to brown so it will not burn on the bottom.) Transfer to a large bowl; refrigerate until just firm enough to beat with an electric mixer, about 45 minutes. (Brown bits will sink to the bottom.)

Preheat oven to 350°. Beat butter at low speed with an electric mixer until smooth and well blended. Add flour, confectioners' sugar, and salt; beat at low speed until blended. (Mixture may appear finely crumbled.)

Press dough evenly into bottom of prepared pan. Bake until crust is golden brown, about 15 minutes. Reduce oven temperature to 300°.

FILLING In a large bowl, whisk together eggs, egg yolk, and salt. Whisk in sugar and flour until smooth. Whisk in lemon zest and juice, whisking until combined.

When crust is done, gently pour filling mixture over hot crust. Bake until center is set, 48 to 50 minutes.

Let cool on a wire rack. Cover, and refrigerate overnight. Cut lemon bars into squares, and dust with confectioners' sugar before serving.

MAKES 6 SERVINGS

CRUST
3/4 cup unsalted butter
1½ cups all-purpose flour
½ cup confectioners' sugar
¼ teaspoon salt

FILLING
6 large eggs
1 large egg yolk
Pinch of salt
2¼ cups sugar
½ cup all-purpose flour
Zest of 1 lemon
1¼ cups fresh lemon juice

Sifted confectioners' sugar

Strawberry Mousse Ladyfingers

3 (3-ounce) packages
soft ladyfingers
2 (8-ounce) packages
cream cheese,
softened
1 cup frozen whipped
topping, thawed
½ cup minced fresh
strawberries
½ cup confectioners'
sugar
¼ cup sour cream
1 (10.75-ounce) all-
butter pound cake*
⅓ cup orange juice
Garnish: 8 whole
strawberries

*We used Sara Lee
All Butter Pound Cake.

Preheat oven to 350°. Place ladyfingers on parchment paper–lined baking sheets. Bake for 2 to 3 minutes or until very lightly toasted. Set aside. In a medium bowl, stir together cream cheese, whipped topping, minced strawberries, confectioners' sugar, and sour cream. Refrigerate until ready to use.

Slice pound cake lengthwise into long ¼-inch-thick slices. Using a 2½-inch round cutter, cut 8 circles of cake. Set aside. Cut one rounded end off ladyfingers so that they measure 2¼ inches long.

To assemble desserts, place a cake round in the center of a 3½-inch ring mold. Brush inside surfaces of ladyfingers lightly with orange juice. Stand rounded end up inside ring mold around cake circle.

Spoon about ⅓ cup mousse into mold. Repeat with remaining cake rounds, ladyfingers, orange juice, and mousse. Refrigerate until ready to serve. To serve, remove ring mold, and tie with a pretty ribbon. Garnish each with a whole strawberry.

Lady fingers are one of the oldest and most delicate of sponge cakes, and they originate from the House of Savoy in 11th-century France. Specialty desserts using the cake were as popular in the courts of Versailles as they are today.

Divinity

In a small saucepan, combine sugar, ½ cup water, and corn syrup. Cook, stirring occasionally, over medium-high heat until a candy thermometer registers 234°.

Meanwhile, in the work bowl of a heavy-duty stand mixer, beat egg whites at high speed until stiff peaks form. With mixer running, gradually pour half of hot sugar mixture over beaten egg whites. Reduce mixer speed to low.

Cook remaining sugar mixture over medium-high heat until a candy thermometer registers 295°. Gradually pour remaining syrup over egg white mixture. Increase mixer speed to high, and beat for 10 minutes or until mixture just begins to lose its glossy appearance.

Working quickly, drop mixture by tablespoons onto parchment paper. Let stand until set.

Store candy in airtight containers for up to 1 week.

MAKES 2 DOZEN

2½ cups sugar
½ cup water
½ cup light corn syrup
3 egg whites

Divinity became a popular treat in the early 20th century with the invention of Karo corn syrup. The recipe was developed to market the introduction of the now-famous syrup.

Miniature Cherry Custard Pies

1 (21-ounce) can cherry pie filling
1 large egg
¼ cup honey
Zest and juice of 1 lemon
1 teaspoon vanilla extract
½ teaspoon ground cardamom
½ teaspoon ground cinnamon
1 (14.1-ounce) package refrigerated pie crusts
Garnish: whipped cream, fresh blueberries

Preheat oven to 350°. Spray 4 (6-ounce) mini pie pans or ceramic dishes with nonstick cooking spray.

In a medium bowl, stir together pie filling, egg, honey, lemon zest and juice, vanilla, cardamom, and cinnamon. Cut 6 (5-inch) circles from pie crusts; reroll remaining dough, and cut 2 more circles.

Place 1 circle in the bottom of each mini pie pan. Divide filling evenly among pie crusts. Using a small star-shaped cookie cutter or a knife, cut a star in the center of each remaining circle.

Place dough over pans, pressing to seal edges. Place on a baking sheet, and bake for 25 minutes or until crust is lightly browned and filling is hot and bubbly. Let cool slightly on a wire rack before serving. Serve with whipped cream and fresh blueberries, if desired.

Miniature desserts are easy to cook now as pans have been specially made in small sizes just for this purpose. These tiny treats insure all of your guests receive their fair share of the crust.

Mini Citrus Bundt Cakes

Preheat oven to 350°. Spray 1 (6-cup) mini Bundt pan with nonstick baking spray with flour.

In the bowl of a stand mixer fitted with the paddle attachment, combine cake mix, egg whites, oil, 1 cup water, and lime juice. Beat at medium speed for 2 minutes or until smooth.

Pour evenly into prepared Bundt pan. Bake for 25 minutes or until a wooden pick inserted in center comes out clean. Let cool in pans for 10 minutes. Remove from pans, and let cool completely on a wire rack. Drizzle with Citrus Cream Cheese Icing. Garnish with lemon and lime zest and lime curls, if desired.

CITRUS CREAM CHEESE ICING In the bowl of a stand mixer fitted with the whip attachment, beat together butter and cream cheese at high speed until creamy.

Add confectioners' sugar, lime juice, and ¼ cup water. Beat at medium speed until combined. Add more water, 1 tablespoon at a time, until icing is pourable but thickly coats the back of a spoon.

MAKES 6 CAKES

1 (18.25-ounce) box white cake mix*
3 large egg whites
¼ cup canola oil
1 cup water
Juice of 1 lime
Citrus Cream Cheese Icing (recipe follows)
Garnish: lemon zest, lime zest, lime curls

We used Duncan Hines White Cake Mix.

CITRUS CREAM CHEESE ICING
MAKES ABOUT 4 CUPS

½ cup butter, softened
4 ounces cream cheese, softened
3 cups confectioners' sugar
¼ cup lime juice
¼ cup water, or more as needed

Lemon and Lime
Icebox Parfaits

1 (16-ounce) purchased angel food cake
2 (10-ounce) jars Dickinson's Lemon Curd
2 (10-ounce) jars Dickinson's Lime Curd
1 (8-ounce) container frozen whipped topping, thawed
Garnish: lemon gumdrops

Using a serrated knife, slice cake horizontally into thirds, trimming any browned edges from cake. Using round cutters, cut cake rounds to fit desired glass. Layer cake, curds, and whipped topping; repeat as desired. Place remaining whipped topping into a pastry bag fitted with a star tip. Pipe a rosette onto each parfait. Garnish with lemon gumdrops, if desired.

Note: You can make ahead and refrigerate.

FOR VARIATIONS OF THE PARFAITS CONSIDER
• using a white cake
• adding coconut or nuts to the top
• drizzling lemon liqueur over the cake
(for an adult version)
• replacing the curd with fresh berries

Single-serving desserts are easy for any hostess to prepare and serve, especially when the filling is purchased curd. Be creative in adding fruits and bite-size pieces of cake to your parfaits.

Jo's Whipping Cream Pound Cake

Preheat oven to 325°. Spray 6 to 8 ovenproof teacups or ramekins with nonstick baking spray with flour.

In a large bowl, beat butter and sugar at medium speed with an electric mixer until fluffy. Add eggs, one at a time, beating well after each addition.

Add flour to butter mixture, alternately with cream, beginning and ending with flour. Add vanilla; beat for 4 minutes. Pour batter into prepared ramekins. Bake for 20 to 25 minutes or until a wooden pick inserted into center comes out clean. Let cool in ramekins. Top with sweetened whipped cream and strawberry halves, if desired.

Tip: For best results, butter and eggs should be at room temperature.

Note: Recipe can be baked at 325° in a tube pan for an hour to 1 hour and 15 minutes or until a wooden pick inserted into center comes out clean.

MAKES 6 TO 8 SMALL CAKES

1 cup butter, softened
3 cups sugar
5 large eggs
3 cups cake flour
1 (½-pint) carton whipping cream, not whipped
1½ teaspoons vanilla extract
Garnish: sweetened whipped cream, strawberry halves

"Miss Jo was the pound cake lady at our church. She gave me my first gorgeous cake plate and every day delivered one of her right-out-of-the-oven warm pound cakes to a lucky recipient; oftentimes it was me. Her recipe will be your favorite, just as it is mine."

– PHYLLIS HOFFMAN DEPIANO

Caramel Apple Tart

1 (9-INCH) TART

½ **(15-ounce) package
   refrigerated pie crusts**
2 **Granny Smith apples,
   sliced to ⅛-inch
   thickness**
2 **Gala apples, sliced to
   ⅛-inch thickness**
¼ **cup honey, warmed**
2 **tablespoons fresh
   lemon juice**
¾ **cup sugar**
¼ **cup cornstarch**
½ **teaspoon ground
   cinnamon**
½ **teaspoon ground
   cardamom**
⅛ **teaspoon salt**
Melted caramel
**Garnish: chopped
   pecans**

Preheat oven to 400°. Fit pie crust into a 9-inch removable-bottom tart pan.

In a medium bowl, combine apples, honey, and lemon juice.

In a separate medium bowl, combine sugar, cornstarch, cinnamon, cardamom, and salt.

Combine sugar mixture with apple mixture; toss gently to coat.

Arrange apples in concentric circles in prepared crust; pour any remaining sugar mixture over apples. Bake for 30 to 35 minutes or until lightly browned.

Let cool in pan for 10 minutes; remove from pan, and let cool completely. Drizzle with melted caramel. Garnish with pecans, if desired.

Apples and spices are the basis of this marvelous tart. Who can resist this magnificent dessert when served with tea?

Raspberry-White Chocolate Tartlets

Preheat oven to 350°.

In a medium bowl, combine cookies, macadamia nuts, ¼ cup granulated sugar, and melted butter. Add egg white, stirring to combine well. Press crumb mixture into bottom and three-fourths up sides of 2 (12-cup) mini cheesecake pans. Bake for 10 minutes. Let cool in pan completely.

In a small microwave-safe bowl, combine 2 tablespoons cold water and gelatin; let stand 5 minutes. Microwave on HIGH until dissolved (approximately 15 seconds total); let cool slightly.

In a medium bowl, combine cream cheese, butter, raspberry preserves, and raspberry extract. Beat at medium speed with an electric mixer until creamy. Add confectioners' sugar, beating to mix well; set aside.

In a separate bowl, beat cream and remaining 1 tablespoon granulated sugar at high speed until soft peaks form. Beat in dissolved gelatin until stiff peaks form. Fold whipped cream mixture into cream cheese mixture until well combined. Fold in white chocolate.

Spoon or pipe mixture into prepared crusts; cover, and chill for 1 to 2 hours. Carefully remove tartlets from pans. Garnish with raspberries, pink sugar, and sugared flowers, if desired.

3 cups crushed shortbread cookies
1¼ cups very finely chopped honey-roasted macadamia nuts
¼ cup plus 1 tablespoon granulated sugar, divided
3 tablespoons butter, melted
1 egg white, lightly beaten
2 tablespoons cold water
1 teaspoon unflavored gelatin
1 (3-ounce) package cream cheese, softened
2 tablespoons unsalted butter, softened
3 tablespoons seedless raspberry preserves, melted
1 teaspoon raspberry extract
½ cup confectioners' sugar
¾ cup heavy whipping cream
⅓ cup finely chopped white chocolate
Garnish: fresh raspberries, pink sugar, sugared flowers

Pecan-Toffee Brownies

1 cup butter
5 (1-ounce) squares
    unsweetened
    chocolate, chopped
2 cups sugar
5 large eggs
2 cups all-purpose flour
½ teaspoon salt
1 teaspoon vanilla extract
1 cup chopped pecans
½ cup toffee bits

Preheat oven to 350°.

Line a 13x9-inch baking pan with heavy-duty aluminum foil.

In a small microwave-safe bowl, melt butter and chocolate in microwave on HIGH in 30-second intervals, stirring between each, until melted and smooth (about 1½ minutes total).

In a large bowl, combine chocolate mixture and sugar. Beat at medium speed with an electric mixer until well blended. Add eggs, one at a time, beating well after each addition. Add flour, salt, and vanilla, beating until just combined.

Spread batter into prepared pan. Bake for 10 minutes.

Sprinkle pecans and toffee bits evenly on top of brownie, and bake 20 to 25 minutes more or until a wooden pick inserted in center comes out still slightly sticky.

Let cool completely in pan on wire rack. Using a serrated knife, cut brownie into 24 squares.

"I would love to meet the person who thought of serving brownies with ice cream. For surely there is a monument somewhere honoring that genius."

– PHYLLIS HOFFMAN DEPIANO

Cranberry-Walnut Tarts

Preheat oven to 350°.

Using a 4-inch round cutter, cut 12 circles from pie crusts.

Press crust into the bottom and up sides of each muffin cup of a 12-cup muffin pan.

In a medium bowl, combine brown sugar, corn syrup, and melted butter, whisking to combine. Add eggs and vanilla, whisking to combine well. Stir in walnuts and cranberries.

Divide mixture evenly among muffin cups. Bake for 20 minutes. Let cool in pan for 5 minutes.

Remove to wire rack, and let cool completely.

MAKES 1 DOZEN

1½ (14.1-ounce) package refrigerated pie crusts
½ cup firmly packed light brown sugar
½ cup dark corn syrup
2 tablespoons butter, melted
2 large eggs
1 teaspoon vanilla extract
1 cup chopped walnuts
¾ cup dried cranberries, finely chopped

Tiny tarts are some of the most enjoyed of all the miniature desserts. Using prepared pie crusts, these small delicacies can be made quickly with a simple walnut and cranberry filling.

Strawberry Baby Cakes with Vanilla-Rose Crème

MAKES 2 DOZEN

1 (16.5-ounce) box white cake mix
1 dry quart strawberries, washed, hulled, and thinly sliced
1 recipe Vanilla-Rose Crème (recipe follows)
Garnish: whole fresh strawberries

VANILLA-ROSE CRÈME
MAKES 2 CUPS

1 envelope unflavored gelatin
3 tablespoons cold water
¼ cup boiling water
2 cups heavy whipping cream
1 tablespoon vanilla extract
1 teaspoon rose water
1 cup confectioners' sugar

Make cake mix according to package directions for a 13x9-inch cake pan. Let cool completely.

Line 2 (12-cup) mini cheesecake pans with parchment strips. Cut 24 (2-inch) rounds from cake. Carefully cut each in half horizontally, leveling for smooth layers, if necessary.

Spoon Vanilla-Rose Crème into a pastry bag fitted with a large round tip. Place a cake-round half in the bottom of each cheesecake well. Line sides of each well with sliced strawberries. Pipe approximately 1 tablespoon Vanilla-Rose Crème into well. Top with remaining cake-round halves. Spread 1 teaspoon Vanilla-Rose Crème on each cake-round half. Refrigerate for 4 hours.

Carefully remove cakes from pan by pushing up each with a pencil or pen. Remove bottom disk, and pull away parchment strips. Pipe a swirl of Vanilla-Rose Crème on each cake.

Garnish with fresh strawberries, if desired. Serve immediately, or refrigerate, covered, for up to 1 day.

VANILLA-ROSE CRÈME In a small bowl, soften gelatin in 3 tablespoons cold water; let stand for 2 minutes. Add ¼ cup boiling water, stirring until gelatin dissolves.

In a large bowl, beat cream, vanilla, rose water, and confectioners' sugar with a mixer at medium-high speed until stiff peaks form. Add gelatin mixture, and beat until combined. Cover, and refrigerate for at least 4 hours or for up to 3 days.

Lemon Pound Cake Squares

Preheat oven to 300°. Spray a 9x5-inch loaf pan with nonstick baking spray with flour.

In the bowl of a stand mixer fitted with the paddle attachment, beat butter and cream cheese at medium-high speed until creamy. Gradually add 1¼ cups sugar, beating until fluffy. Add eggs, one at a time, beating well after each addition. In a large bowl, whisk together flour, lemon zest, and salt. Gradually add flour mixture to butter mixture, beating just until combined.

Pour batter into prepared pan. Bake for 1 hour and 20 minutes to 1 hour and 25 minutes or until a wooden pick inserted in center of cake comes out clean. Let cool in pan for 10 minutes. Remove from pan. Let cool completely on a wire rack.

While pound cake bakes, in a medium saucepan, combine blueberries and remaining ½ cup sugar. Bring to a boil over high heat. Reduce heat to medium-low, and simmer for 15 minutes, stirring occasionally. Stir together 2 tablespoons water and cornstarch; add to blueberry mixture, stirring constantly. Simmer for 3 minutes, stirring occasionally, or until mixture begins to thicken. Remove from heat, and let cool.

Trim edges of cake to form a rectangle. Cut rectangle in half crosswise. Cut each half in half lengthwise. Cut each strip into 3 equal pieces.

Preheat broiler. Brush tops of poundcake squares with melted butter. Broil for 2 minutes or until tops just begin to brown. Top pound-cake squares with blueberry sauce. Garnish with lemon zest, if desired.

MAKES 1 DOZEN

½ **cup butter, softened**
½ **(8-ounce) package cream cheese, softened**
1¾ **cups sugar, divided**
3 **large eggs**
1⅓ **cups all-purpose flour**
2 **teaspoons lemon zest**
¼ **teaspoon salt**
1 **(12-ounce) package frozen blueberries**
2 **tablespoons water**
2 **teaspoons cornstarch**
2 **tablespoons butter, melted**
Garnish: lemon zest

Snowball Spice Cookies

MAKES ABOUT 5 DOZEN

1½ cups pecan halves, toasted and finely chopped
3¼ cups all-purpose flour
1 teaspoon salt
1 teaspoon ground cinnamon
¼ teaspoon ground nutmeg
¼ teaspoon ground cloves
1 cup plus 6 tablespoons unsalted butter, room temperature
1 cup granulated sugar
1 teaspoon vanilla extract
1 cup confectioners' sugar, sifted

Preheat oven to 325°.

In a large bowl, combine pecans, flour, salt, cinnamon, nutmeg, and cloves.

In the bowl of a stand mixer, combine butter and granulated sugar; beat until creamy, about 1 minute. Add flour mixture and vanilla, beating until combined.

Using a tablespoon, scoop out dough, and roll into 1-inch balls. Place on ungreased baking sheets, and bake for 20 minutes or until lightly browned.

Let cool on baking sheets for 3 minutes. Let cool completely on wire racks. Roll in confectioners' sugar.

Petite cookies rolled in confectioners' sugar are impossible to resist. The fragrant aroma of the cookies baking fills the kitchen with the spice trio of cinnamon, cloves, and nutmeg.

Lemon-Almond Cookies

Preheat oven to 325°. Line a baking sheet with parchment paper.

In a medium bowl, beat butter and sugar at medium speed with an electric mixer until fluffy. Add lemonade concentrate, lemon zest, and almond extract, beating until combined. Gradually add flour, beating until combined.

Roll dough into 1-inch balls; place on prepared baking sheet. Using the bottom of a glass dipped in additional sugar, flatten each ball to a 2-inch round. Press sliced almonds firmly into each unbaked cookie. Bake cookies for 14 to 16 minutes or until lightly browned. Let cool for 2 minutes; remove to wire racks, and let cool completely. Store in an airtight container.

MAKES 2 DOZEN

- **½ cup unsalted butter, softened**
- **¾ cup sugar**
- **2 tablespoons frozen lemonade concentrate, thawed**
- **2 teaspoons grated lemon zest**
- **¼ teaspoon almond extract**
- **1½ cups self-rising flour**
- **Additional sugar**
- **Sliced almonds**

Lemon-Almond Cookies are very refreshing when paired with tea. The almond slices can be artfully arranged on top of the cookies, making them beautiful in addition to delicious.

Lemon-Buttermilk Ice Cream Sandwiches

MAKES 1½ DOZEN

Buttermilk Ice Cream
  (recipe follows)
Lemon Cookies
  (recipe follows)

BUTTERMILK ICE CREAM
MAKES ABOUT 3 QUARTS

2 cups heavy whipping
  cream
2 (14-ounce) cans
  sweetened
  condensed milk
1 quart whole buttermilk
1 tablespoon fresh
  lemon juice
1 vanilla bean, split and
  scraped, seeds
  reserved

LEMON COOKIES
MAKES 3 DOZEN
  (3-INCH) COOKIES

2 cups butter, softened
2 cups sugar
3 large eggs
2 tablespoons lemon zest
¼ cup fresh lemon juice
5 cups all-purpose flour
2 teaspoons baking
  powder
½ teaspoon salt

Using an ice-cream scoop, place 1 scoop of Buttermilk Ice Cream on flat side of half of Lemon Cookies. Place remaining cookies flat side down on ice cream. Store in freezer in an airtight container until ready to serve.

BUTTERMILK ICE CREAM In a large bowl, beat cream at medium-high speed with an electric mixer until soft peaks form. Add sweetened condensed milk; beat for 2 minutes. Add buttermilk, lemon juice, and vanilla bean seeds.

Pour mixture into the container of an ice cream freezer. Freeze according to manufacturer's instructions. Ice cream will be soft. For a firmer texture, spoon ice cream into a freezer-safe container, and freeze for up to 1 month.

LEMON COOKIES In a large bowl, beat butter and sugar at medium speed with an electric mixer until creamy. Add eggs, one at a time, beating after each addition. Beat in lemon zest and juice.

In a medium bowl, combine flour, baking powder, and salt. Gradually add flour mixture to butter mixture, beating to combine well. Divide dough in half. Press each half of dough into a disk, and wrap tightly in plastic wrap. Refrigerate dough for 1 hour.

Preheat oven to 350°. Line 2 baking sheets with parchment paper. On a lightly floured surface, roll dough to ¼-inch thickness. Using a 3-inch flower-shaped cookie cutter, cut out dough. Place on prepared pan, 2 inches apart. Bake for 12 to 14 minutes. Let cool on pan for 2 minutes. Let cool completely on wire racks.

Fresh Fruit Tarts

Preheat oven to 450°.

On a lightly floured surface, unroll crusts. Using a 4½-inch round cutter, cut 6 circles from each pie crust. Line 12 (4-inch) tart pans with prepared crusts; prick bottoms of crusts with fork. Place on baking sheet, and bake for 7 to 8 minutes or until golden brown. Let cool on wire racks for 5 minutes; remove from pans, and let cool completely.

In a medium bowl, combine cream cheese, ¼ cup honey, and lemon zest and juice. Beat at medium speed with an electric mixer until creamy. Add confectioners' sugar, beating until combined.

Spoon cream cheese mixture into prepared crusts. Top with strawberries, kiwi, blueberries, and raspberries.

In a small bowl, heat remaining 2 tablespoons honey in microwave on HIGH for 15 seconds or until melted. Using a small pastry brush, brush honey on fruit.

MAKES 1 DOZEN

1 (14.1-ounce) package refrigerated pie crusts
2 (8-ounce) packages cream cheese, softened
¼ cup plus 2 tablespoons honey, divided
2 tablespoons lemon zest
2 tablespoons fresh lemon juice
½ cup confectioners' sugar
1 (1-pound) container fresh strawberries, sliced
4 kiwi, sliced into quarters
1 cup fresh blueberries
1 cup fresh raspberries

The delicate crusts of these small tarts cradle an ensemble of fresh fruits combined with a cream cheese filling. Create your own combination of fruits in season, and make this recipe your own.

Molasses-Walnut Tarts

MAKES 1 DOZEN

1½ (14.1-ounce) packages
    refrigerated pie
    crusts
1 cup firmly packed light
    brown sugar
½ cup molasses
½ cup dark corn syrup
¼ cup butter, melted
3 large eggs
2 teaspoons vanilla
    extract
¼ teaspoon salt
1¾ cups finely chopped
    walnuts

Preheat oven to 350°.

On a lightly floured surface, unroll crusts. Using a 4-inch round cutter, cut 12 circles from pie crusts. Line 12 (3½-inch) removable-bottom tart pans with crusts; prick bottoms of crusts with a fork. Place on a baking sheet, and bake for 5 minutes.

In a medium bowl, combine brown sugar, molasses, and corn syrup. Whisk in melted butter and eggs until well combined. Whisk in vanilla and salt. Stir in walnuts. Evenly divide filling between prepared crusts. Bake for 20 to 22 minutes or until lightly browned and center is set.

"Walnuts are considered to be one of the healthiest additions to one's diet. And when cooked into a tart, they are considered to be one of the most delicious additions to one's diet. That gives me two reasons to make these tarts for my guests."

– PHYLLIS HOFFMAN DEPIANO

Chocolate-Peanut Butter Bars

Preheat oven to 350°. Line a 13x9-inch baking pan with heavy-duty aluminum foil; spray foil with nonstick cooking spray.

In a medium bowl, combine butter and chocolate. Microwave on HIGH in 30-second intervals, stirring between each, until melted and smooth (about 1½ minutes total).

In a large bowl, combine sugar, eggs, and vanilla. Beat at medium speed with an electric mixer until combined. Add chocolate mixture to sugar mixture, beating to mix well.

In a separate bowl, sift together flour, cocoa powder, and salt. Gradually add flour mixture to sugar mixture, beating to combine well. Spread batter evenly into prepared pan. Bake for 14 to 16 minutes or until set in center. Let cool in pan for 10 minutes.

With greased hands, press Peanut Butter Filling evenly on top of brownie in pan. Place in freezer for 15 minutes. Spread melted chocolate on top of peanut butter filling. Sprinkle with peanuts. Let stand until set.

PEANUT BUTTER FILLING In a medium bowl, combine peanut butter and butter. Beat at medium speed with an electric mixer until creamy. Gradually add confectioners' sugar, beating until smooth. Beat in vanilla.

MAKES ABOUT 3 DOZEN

1 cup butter
5 (1-ounce) squares semisweet chocolate, chopped
1 cup sugar
4 large eggs
1½ teaspoons vanilla extract
1¼ cups all-purpose flour
2 tablespoons unsweetened cocoa powder
¼ teaspoon salt
Peanut Butter Filling (recipe follows)
1 (12-ounce) bag semisweet chocolate morsels, melted
½ cup chopped salted roasted peanuts

PEANUT BUTTER FILLING
MAKES ABOUT 3 CUPS

1½ cups creamy peanut butter
½ cup butter, softened
2 cups confectioners' sugar
1 teaspoon vanilla extract

Cookies and Cream Truffles

MAKES ABOUT 2 DOZEN

2 (8-ounce) packages cream cheese, softened
⅓ cup confectioners' sugar
1 cup cream-filled chocolate sandwich cookie crumbs (about 10 cookies crushed)
1 (1-pound) package vanilla-flavored candy coating, melted
Garnish: cream-filled chocolate cookie crumbs

In a medium bowl, combine cream cheese and confectioners' sugar. Beat at medium speed with an electric mixer until creamy. Add cookie crumbs, beating to combine. Cover, and chill for 2 hours.

Roll cream cheese mixture into 1-inch balls, and place on a baking sheet lined with parchment paper. Freeze for 4 hours or up to overnight.

Using wooden picks, dip each ball into candy coating. Garnish tops with additional cookie crumbs, if desired.

Make-ahead recipes are always pleasing to hostesses and make preparing for a tea much easier. Using the candy coatings that are available to purchase, simply melt the coating and dip your confection into it to prepare these truffles with ease.

Dark Chocolate and Sea Salt-Topped Green Tea Shortbread

Preheat oven to 325°. Line a 13x9-inch baking pan with parchment paper, allowing parchment paper to extend over sides of pan.

In the bowl of a stand mixer fitted with the paddle attachment, beat butter, confectioners' sugar, matcha powder, salt, and vanilla at medium-high speed until creamy, about 1 minute. Add flour; beating just until combined (dough will be crumbly).

Press dough into prepared pan. Bake for 15 to 17 minutes or until edges are lightly browned. Let cool completely in pan on a wire rack. Using parchment as handles, lift shortbread from pan. In a small microwavable bowl, place all but 2 tablespoons chopped chocolate.

Microwave on HIGH in 20-second intervals, stirring between each, until melted and smooth (about 1 minute total). Stir in reserved chocolate until melted and smooth, and spread over shortbread. Sprinkle with sea salt. Let cool completely, about 30 minutes. Cut into 16 squares.

MAKES 14 TO 16 SERVINGS

- **1 cup butter, softened**
- **1 cup confectioners' sugar**
- **2 tablespoons matcha powder***
- **½ teaspoon salt**
- **½ teaspoon vanilla extract**
- **2 cups all-purpose flour**
- **2 (4-ounce) bars dark chocolate, chopped**
- **1 teaspoon sea salt**

Matcha is a Japanese powdered green tea. You can find it at specialty tea shops or online.

Surprise your guests with a green tea shortbread hiding beneath a luxurious layer of sea salt-topped dark chocolate.

Sweetheart Chocolate Cakes

MAKES 6 SERVINGS

1/4 **cup granulated sugar, divided**

1 3/4 **cups all-purpose flour**

3/4 **cup unsweetened cocoa powder**

1 1/2 **teaspoons baking soda**

1 **teaspoon ground cinnamon**

3/4 **teaspoon salt**

2/3 **cup butter, softened**

1 1/2 **cups firmly packed light brown sugar**

2 **large eggs**

1 **(16-ounce) container sour cream**

1 **teaspoon vanilla extract**

Garnish: confectioners' sugar

Preheat oven to 350°. Spray 6 (2-cup) ramekins with nonstick cooking spray. Dust each with granulated sugar, tilting to evenly coat bottom and sides of ramekins; discard excess.

In a medium bowl, whisk together flour, cocoa, baking soda, cinnamon, and salt. In a large bowl, beat butter and brown sugar at medium speed with an electric mixer until fluffy. Add eggs, one at a time, beating until blended. Beat in sour cream and vanilla. Beat in flour mixture just until smooth. Divide batter evenly among prepared ramekins. Use a small spatula to smooth tops of batter.

Bake for 40 to 45 minutes or until a wooden pick inserted in centers comes out clean. Let cool in ramekins for 10 minutes on a wire rack; serve warm. Garnish with confectioners' sugar, if desired.

Nothing says "I love you" like a delectable chocolate dessert, especially when it is decorated with a heart. Simply cut out a paper heart to fit inside your dish. Place it on the cake, sprinkle with confectioners' sugar, and remove the paper heart.

Heart Sandwich Cookies

In a medium bowl, whisk together flour, baking powder, cinnamon, and salt. In a large bowl, beat butter and sugar at medium speed with an electric mixer until creamy.

Add egg and vanilla; beat until combined. Beat in flour mixture until combined. Form into 2 disks, and wrap with plastic wrap; refrigerate for 2 hours or until firm. Preheat oven to 350°. Line 3 baking sheets with parchment paper.

On a lightly floured surface, roll half of dough to ¼-inch thickness. Using a linzer cookie cutter fitted with the heart cutout, cut out 24 cookies. Carefully transfer to prepared baking sheets. Remove heart cutout from linzer cookie cutter, and repeat process with remaining dough.

Bake cookies for 10 minutes or until edges are lightly browned.

Let cool completely on sheets on wire racks. Spread whole cookies with 2 teaspoons jam, then top with cutout cookies. Garnish with confectioners' sugar, if desired.

MAKES ABOUT 2 DOZEN

3 cups all-purpose flour
1 teaspoon baking
powder
1 teaspoon ground
cinnamon
¼ teaspoon salt
1 cup butter, softened
1 cup sugar
1 large egg
1 teaspoon vanilla
extract
1 cup strawberry jam,
warmed slightly
Garnish: confectioners'
sugar

The beauty of tea food is part of the wonderful experience of tea. These delicate heart cookies with strawberry filling peeking through are works of art. While they look complicated, they are actually easily made using a linzer cookie cutter.

Donnelley Tarts

1 cup chocolate graham-cracker crumbs

½ cup cream-filled chocolate sandwich cookie crumbs, cream removed

3 tablespoons butter, melted

1 egg white

1 tablespoon firmly packed brown sugar

⅛ teaspoon salt

1 teaspoon unflavored gelatin

2 tablespoons cold water

3 tablespoons boiling water

1 cup heavy whipping cream

¼ cup granulated sugar

3 tablespoons Irish cream liqueur

Garnish: chopped pistachios, spiral cream-filled wafer cookies

Preheat oven to 325°.

In a small bowl, combine graham-cracker crumbs, cookie crumbs, butter, egg white, brown sugar, and salt.

Press into bottom and halfway up sides of a 12-cup mini-cheesecake pan. Bake for 8 minutes.

In a small bowl, soften gelatin in 2 tablespoons cold water; let stand for 2 minutes.

Add 3 tablespoons boiling water, stirring until gelatin dissolves.

In a medium bowl, beat cream at medium speed with an electric mixer until foamy; gradually add granulated sugar, beating until soft peaks form.

Gently stir in liqueur. Add gelatin mixture, stirring gently. Cover, and chill for 2 hours. Pipe mousse evenly into chocolate shells. Garnish with chopped pistachios and cream-filled wafer cookies, if desired.

Chocolate-Strawberry Brownie Bites

Preheat oven to 350°. Spray a 9-inch square baking pan with cooking spray.

Bake brownie mix according to package directions. Let cool completely in pan.

In another medium bowl, combine butter and strawberry purée. Beat at medium speed with an electric mixer until smooth. Add confectioners' sugar, and beat until smooth.

Remove brownie from pan. Cut into 30 squares. Split each square in half crosswise. Pipe or spread strawberry frosting onto the bottoms of the brownies, and cover with the tops. Pipe or spread a small dollop of frosting on the top of each brownie. Garnish with fresh strawberries, if desired.

MAKES 30 BITES

1 (18.3-ounce) box fudge brownie mix
¼ cup butter, softened
½ cup strawberry purée
2½ cups confectioners' sugar
Garnish: fresh strawberries

The chocolate and strawberry flavor duo transforms basic brownies into a decadent dessert. Don't tell anyone how simple it is to make; only you will know!

Orange-Date Pinwheels

DOUGH

1 cup butter, softened
1 cup granulated sugar
1 cup firmly packed light
    brown sugar
3 large eggs
1 teaspoon orange zest
4¼ cups all-purpose
    flour
½ teaspoon baking soda
½ teaspoon salt

FILLING

1 (10-ounce) package
    pitted dates,
    finely chopped
1 cup fresh orange juice
¼ cup sugar
½ teaspoon ground
    cinnamon

DOUGH In a large bowl, beat butter and sugars at medium speed with an electric mixer until fluffy. Add eggs, one at a time, beating well after each addition. Beat in orange zest. In a small bowl, combine flour, baking soda, and salt. Gradually add flour mixture to butter mixture, beating until combined. Divide dough in half, and wrap each half tightly in plastic wrap. Refrigerate for 2 hours.

FILLING In a medium saucepan, combine dates, orange juice, sugar, and cinnamon. Cook over medium heat, stirring frequently, for 8 to 10 minutes or until mixture is very thick; let cool for 30 minutes.

To assemble cookies: On a lightly floured surface, roll half of dough into a 14x10-inch rectangle. Spread half of date mixture evenly over dough. Starting with long side, roll up dough, jelly-roll style, to form a log. Wrap log in parchment paper. Repeat procedure with remaining dough and date mixture. Freeze for 2 hours or up to overnight.

Preheat oven to 375°. Line baking sheets with parchment paper.

Remove 1 log from freezer. Slice into ½-inch-thick slices. Place on prepared baking sheets, and bake for 16 to 18 minutes or until lightly browned. Let cool on pans for 2 minutes. Remove from pans, and let cool completely on wire racks. Repeat with remaining log.

Mini Orange and Chocolate Cheesecakes

Preheat oven to 350°.

In a small bowl, combine cracker crumbs, 6 tablespoons sugar, melted butter, and egg white. Press mixture into bottom and halfway up sides of 3 (12-cup) mini cheesecake pans. Bake for 8 minutes.

In a large bowl, beat cream cheese and remaining 1 cup sugar at medium speed with an electric mixer until creamy. Beat in eggs, orange zest and juice, and flour until batter is smooth. Spoon evenly into prepared crusts.

Bake for 16 to 18 minutes or until set. (Can be made ahead and frozen.) Garnish with whipped cream and orange zest, if desired.

MAKES 3 DOZEN

- 3 cups chocolate graham-cracker crumbs
- 1 cup plus 6 tablespoons sugar, divided
- 3/4 cup butter, melted
- 1 large egg white, lightly beaten
- 2 (8-ounce) packages cream cheese, softened
- 2 large eggs
- 2 tablespoons orange zest
- 1/4 cup fresh orange juice
- 2 tablespoons all-purpose flour
- Garnish: fresh whipped cream, orange zest

Cheesecake is one of the most popular desserts in the world. Its origins date back 4,000 years to ancient Greece. It was not until the late 1800s in the United States when cream cheese was made and used instead of other types of cheeses. The orange and chocolate miniature cakes combine two interesting flavors for a unique treat.

Pumpkin Trifles

MAKES 8 SERVINGS

1 cup canned pumpkin
1 (8-ounce) container
    frozen nondairy
    whipped topping,
    thawed and divided
1 cup confectioners'
    sugar, divided
1½ teaspoons pumpkin
    pie spice
½ teaspoon ground
    cinnamon
½ teaspoon salt
1 (8-ounce) package
    cream cheese, softened
2 teaspoons vanilla extract
1 cup gingersnap cookie
    crumbs
Garnish: whipped cream,
    pumpkin pie
    spice, gingersnaps

In a medium bowl, combine pumpkin, ½ container whipped topping, ½ cup confectioners' sugar, pumpkin pie spice, cinnamon, and salt. Beat at medium speed with an electric mixer until well combined; set aside.

In a medium bowl, combine cream cheese, remaining ½ container whipped topping, remaining ½ cup confectioners' sugar, and vanilla. Beat at medium speed with an electric mixer until smooth.

In small glasses, layer cream cheese mixture, gingersnap cookie crumbs, and pumpkin mixture. Garnish with whipped cream, pumpkin pie spice, and gingersnaps, if desired.

"I made my first trifle years ago from a recipe from Williamsburg, Virginia, that was popular in colonial times. Each layer that is added to a trifle is like adding an instrument to the orchestra, creating a masterful symphony of flavors."

– PHYLLIS HOFFMAN DEPIANO

Blackstrap Biscuits

Preheat oven to 325°.

In a small bowl, combine flour, baking soda, salt, and cinnamon.

In a large bowl, beat brown sugar and butter at medium speed with an electric mixer until creamy. Add egg, molasses, and vanilla; beat until smooth. Gradually add flour mixture, beating at low speed. Wrap dough in plastic wrap; refrigerate for 2 hours.

Using a tablespoon measure, drop batter on an ungreased baking sheet, 1½ inches apart. Bake for 12 minutes. Cool 1 minute on baking sheet. Using a 3-inch shamrock-shaped cutter, cut baked biscuits into shamrocks.

To assemble, spread an even layer of Creamy Maple Filling on flat side of one biscuit; place another biscuit on top, pressing together gently. Repeat with remaining biscuits. Lightly dust frosted edges of cookies with green castor sugar, if desired.

CREAMY MAPLE FILLING In a medium bowl, beat butter, maple syrup, and vanilla at medium speed with an electric mixer until smooth.

Gradually add confectioners' sugar and brown sugar, beating until creamy.

MAKES 1 DOZEN

- **1½ cups all-purpose flour**
- **½ teaspoon baking soda**
- **½ teaspoon salt**
- **¼ teaspoon ground cinnamon**
- **1 cup firmly packed brown sugar**
- **½ cup unsalted butter, softened**
- **1 large egg**
- **¼ cup blackstrap molasses**
- **1 teaspoon vanilla extract**
- **1 recipe Creamy Maple Filling (recipe follows)**
- **Garnish: green castor sugar**

CREAMY MAPLE FILLING
MAKES 1½ CUPS

- **¾ cup butter, softened**
- **3 tablespoons maple syrup**
- **1 teaspoon vanilla extract**
- **1¾ cups confectioners' sugar**
- **¼ cup firmly packed brown sugar**

Praline Cannoli

½ cup firmly packed
   dark brown sugar
1¾ cup heavy whipping
   cream, divided
2 tablespoons butter
½ teaspoon vanilla
   extract
½ cup toffee bits
42 mini cannoli shells*
Garnish: melted
   caramel, finely
   chopped pecans

*We used Cannoli di Sicilia
brand mini cannoli shells
from ditalia.com.

In a small saucepan, combine brown sugar, ¼ cup cream, and butter over medium heat. Cook for 3 to 4 minutes, stirring constantly, until sugar dissolves. Stir in vanilla; let cool completely.

In a medium bowl, beat remaining 1½ cups cream at high speed with an electric mixer until stiff peaks form. Fold in brown sugar mixture and toffee bits. Pipe mixture into cannoli shells. Drizzle with melted caramel, and sprinkle with chopped pecans, if desired.

Who can resist the crunchy delight of a cannoli? Ready-to-fill cannoli can be purchased and filled to take the challenging part out of making this dessert. You just make the praline filling, fill the shell, and garnish.

S'more Cupcakes

Preheat oven to 350°. Line 2 (12-cup) muffin pans with paper liners; set aside.

In a large bowl, combine butter, cream cheese, and sugar. Beat at high speed with an electric mixer until fluffy. Add eggs, one at a time, beating well after each addition.

In a medium bowl, sift together flours, baking powder, and salt. Add flour mixture to butter mixture alternately with milk, beginning and ending with flour mixture. Beat in vanilla. Spoon batter into muffin cups, filling about two-thirds full. Bake for 18 to 20 minutes or until a wooden pick inserted in centers comes out clean; let cool completely.

Using a melon baller, remove center of each cupcake, leaving bottom intact. (Discard or reserve cupcake scraps for another use.) Pipe marshmallow fluff into the center of each cupcake. Ice tops of cupcakes with Chocolate Fudge Icing. Garnish with miniature marshmallows and graham crackers, if desired.

CHOCOLATE FUDGE ICING In a medium saucepan, combine granulated sugar, brown sugar, and cream. Bring to a boil over medium-high heat; reduce heat to medium-low, and simmer for 6 minutes, stirring frequently.

Remove from heat; add chocolate and butter, stirring until melted and smooth.

Let cool for 10 minutes. Gradually whisk in confectioners' sugar. Refrigerate for 1 to 1½ hours, whisking occasionally, until chocolate mixture reaches spreadable consistency.

MAKES 2 DOZEN

- ½ cup unsalted butter, softened
- 1 (8-ounce) package cream cheese, softened
- 1½ cups sugar
- 4 large eggs
- 2 cups cake flour
- 1 cup whole-wheat-graham flour
- 2½ teaspoons baking powder
- ¼ teaspoon salt
- 1 cup whole milk
- 1 teaspoon vanilla extract
- 2 (7.5-ounce) jars marshmallow fluff
- Chocolate Fudge Icing (recipe follows)
- Garnish: miniature marshmallows, graham crackers

CHOCOLATE FUDGE ICING
MAKES ABOUT 6 CUPS

- 1 cup granulated sugar
- 1 cup firmly packed dark brown sugar
- 2 cups heavy whipping cream
- 8 (1-ounce) squares semisweet chocolate, chopped
- 1¼ cups cold butter, cut into pieces
- 2 cups confectioners' sugar, sifted

Frozen Cake Batter Bonbons

MAKES ABOUT 4 DOZEN

½ cup butter, softened
1 (8-ounce) package
   cream cheese,
   softened
1 (18.25-ounce) box
   white cake mix
3 tablespoons
   strawberry extract
2 pounds vanilla-
   flavored candy
   coating or almond
   bark, melted
Garnish: pink and white
   jimmies

Line 2 baking sheets with parchment paper; set aside.

In a large bowl, beat butter and cream cheese at medium speed with an electric mixer until smooth. Add cake mix and strawberry extract, beating to combine. Cover, and freeze for 2 hours.

Roll cream cheese mixture into 1-inch balls, and place on prepared baking sheets. Using two forks, dip bonbons into melted candy coating, gently shaking off excess. Set bonbons on prepared baking sheets. Sprinkle tops with jimmies, if desired; return to freezer. Serve frozen. Store in freezer in an airtight container for up to 2 weeks.

Just mention the words "cake batter," and we all have memories of begging to lick the bowl when our mothers would bake a cake. Cake batter is a favorite among children, and they will love this frozen treat.

Recipe Index

APPETIZERS

SWEETS

TEAS